HOW TO PLAY

GOLF

HOW TO PLAY
GOLF

ALASDAIR
BARR

Published by Guinness Books
33 London Road
Enfield
Middlesex EN2 6DJ

Produced and Designed by Mander Gooch Callow

Copyright © 1988 Mander Gooch Callow

Illustration: Sharon F. Gower

Printed and bound in Great Britain by
Hazell Watson & Viney Ltd., Aylesbury

British Library Cataloguing in Publication Data

       Barr, Alasdair
        How to play golf.
        1. Golf – Manuals
        1. Title
        796.352'3

ISBN 0-85112-366-X

Contents

Introduction

So you want to play golf. Getting started can seem very complicated with all that appears to be involved in trying to sort out the right equipment, with all its complexities, let alone learning how to play. Hopefully, this book will lead you through the equipment jungle and explain the golf swing and the movements necessary to play well, as well as help you to understand why these movements are important.

The beauty of golf is that there is but one swing and we have golf clubs designed to create different effects, unlike the tennis player who has to provide all the shots with one racquet.

Always try to keep this one swing in mind, as the golfer is the person in charge and he is always the same. The swings with different clubs might appear to be longer or shorter but this is due entirely to the length of the shaft of the club and nothing to do with the player. By understanding the fundamentals required to make the swing, the more advanced player may also be able to spot his faults and save a lot of heartache by quickly getting back on track.

Learning to play golf is a two-phased exercise. The first phase is to learn the movements involved in the swing of the club enabling you to actually strike the ball. The second is to actually play the game around the course. This involves all the different shots, the awkward lies, uphills and downhills, bunker shots, fairway and green side, pitching and putting and playing in adverse weather conditions.

This book will also explain the different types of match that can be played and the handicapping system which makes golf so unique. Which other sport can you play that permits you to play on the same playing surfaces as the superstars and also, with your handicap, compete against them? We will also look at the basic etiquette which has also kept golf apart from other sports.

Incidentally, all directions given are for right-handed players and should of course be reversed if you are left-handed.

GOOD MANNERS

Golf has always managed to retain a good standard of manners and keep itself above the standards set in some other sports. Golf is a game for gentlemen and as the player is his own judge and jury he carries a lot of responsibility to adhere to the rules. The game is a contest between the player and the course rather than a battle between players and as such always try to allow your opponent or partner the consideration you would like yourself.

Equipment

Invariably, when someone decides to start golf, Grandad's clubs are located in the loft, under the illusion that they will do to begin with. If he starts off with these clubs the beginner does himself the greatest disservice, as they will probably be worse than useless. However, this does not mean that he has to invest in a full and expensive set to begin with.

The maximum number of clubs the golfer is allowed to carry is fourteen, but the learner can start quite happily with a half-set. These need not necessarily be expensive, in fact second-hand ones will do at this stage, and will allow you to discover whether golf is the game for you, without breaking the bank.

Whether you choose new or second-hand, the important factor is that the clubs should fit the golfer and not the other way around. If the beginner is not going to waste his money, there are specifications that need to be taken into account such as weight, and very importantly at this stage, club lie, shaft flex and grip thickness. It is therefore essential to seek the advice of a PGA professional. His services are available to everyone whether members of a golf club or not. He will be able to advise on the correct clubs according to these specifications and make any adjustments or refurbishments that are necessary.

The Clubs

In the proposed half-set you will need at least four irons. Choose alternate odd or even numbers but it is probably best to start at the four iron, as the lack of loft on the number three iron makes it slightly more difficult to use.

You will now have irons numbered four, six, eight and wedge (some sets call the wedge a number ten iron, but the degree of loft is exactly the same). In addition a wooden club, ideally a number three is all that is

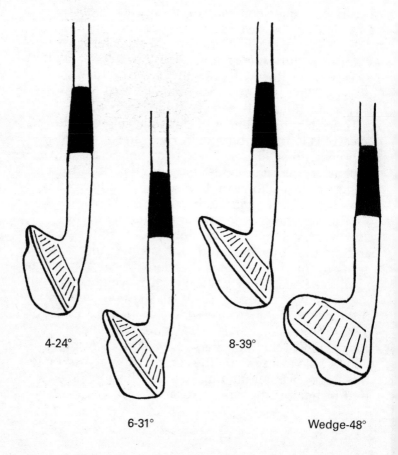

4-24°

6-31°

8-39°

Wedge-48°

required here, as this can double as a club to drive with and use for the longer fairway shots.

Finally you will need to choose a putter.
There are literally thousands of different styles of club so how do you go about choosing one that will be suitable? The professional will go out on to the putting green with you and allow you to try different styles, weights and club lie and with his help and a process of elimination you will arrive at the putter of your choice.

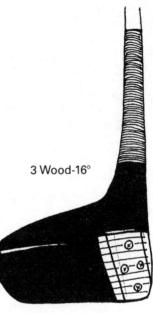

3 Wood-16°

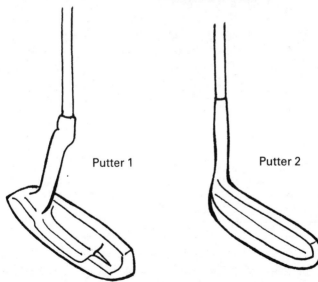

Putter 1

Putter 2

RULE BOOK

In order to play the game and particularly to compete, the golfer must have an understanding of the rules of golf. Doing this will stop him from losing matches through ignorance but also allows him to take advantage of rules that are there to help. It can also stop the players from inadvertently 'cheating' through lack of knowledge.

The rules are many and in some cases quite complicated, so each player should obtain a copy and keep it in his golf bag so that reference can be made to it when required.
It would be impossible to go through all the rules here so they will appear as they tend to crop up in everyday play.

Your putter can be a great friend, as one top tournament player said, "If I have to choose between my wife and my putter, I will miss her!".

While this half-set of combination clubs might seem a little limited, it will allow the beginner to decide whether or not he or she has any ability for the game.

There is a popular misconception among beginners that specific clubs can be made to hit the ball further. This is not so, the length of the shaft and the position of the hands dictates the fullness of the swing and this effects the distance the ball will travel. By moving your hands down the handle you can shorten that distance. For example, if we take the six iron and go down the handle, the swing will automatically become shorter and therefore the ball will not travel so far. As can be seen the less lofted clubs also have longer shafts and this will permit a fuller, freer swing, encouraging a more powerful strike.

The different numbers on the irons indicate the distances for which the clubs are designed. The higher the number of the club, the higher the ball will fly. Therefore as it doesn't spend too much time going forward, it doesn't go so far. So the low numbers are used for the long shots and the high for the short shots. The wedge or ten iron is also used for pitching the ball and at this stage, for bunker shots.

There are three important factors to take into account when buying the clubs.

FAULT-FINDER

It is very difficult to describe feel in words, but guard against the putter that is too heavy, as it will be difficult to swing smoothly and keep the head under control. Equally the putter head that is too light will give no sensation at all when being swung.

Club lie

This is the angle at which the shaft comes from the head when the sole or bottom of the golf club is resting on the grass. It is absolutely vital to have this correct in order to return the club face to the ball at impact, exactly as you placed it behind the ball in the set-up.

If the toe of the club is off the ground then the club face will close, as the heel strikes the ground first. Alternatively, if the heel is off the ground the club face will open as the toe catches the ground. The professional will be able to adjust the club to suit you, once he has positioned you in the correct set-up position.

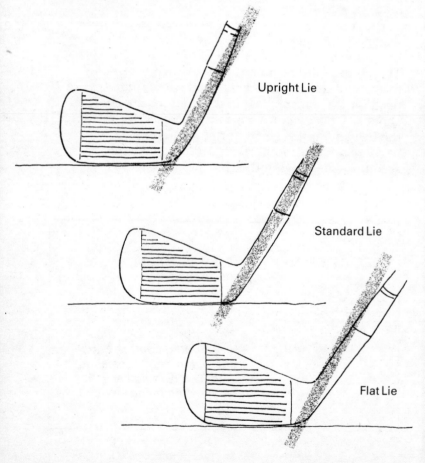

Upright Lie

Standard Lie

Flat Lie

FAULT-FINDER

There is a popular belief that taller people need longer than standard clubs and shorter people, shorter shafts. The length of the golf club has nothing whatsoever to do with the height of the golfer. Most people's bodies are in proportion, so tall people have longer arms. It will ruin your game if you buy clubs on this basis.

The determining factor is how far your clenched fist is from the ground, as that is the distance the club shaft has to cover to meet your hand. In fact an example of how this can work is that Gary Player uses clubs half an inch longer than standard, so it would appear that his arms are a little short, even though he is only approximately 5'7" tall.

Remember, that a club should be fitted to the golfer and not the other way around as this will cause all sorts of problems during the swing. Once again, it should be stressed that the beginner should seek professional advice if he is not to end up with a bag full of scrap metal.

Shaft flex

The shaft flex can be broken down into four main categories – stiff, regular, 'A' and ladies. To denote the shaft flex, manufacturers' put the symbol on a label around the club shaft.

Stiff, marked 'S', is suited to the player with strong hands and an aggressive swing as he does not require any help from the shaft. Regular, marked 'R', is suitable for the average player. The 'A' shaft is suited to the older player. This slightly softer shaft will provide a little more club head speed as the whippiness, or shaft flex, unwinds through the ball and provides that extra little kick.

The ladies', or 'L' shaft, is even softer than the 'A' shaft and this is suited to ladies and children, who don't generate a lot of club head speed. Assistance is provided by the shaft unwinding through the ball.

Grip thickness

It is important to have the right size of grip. If the grip is too thick, the club will be held too much in the palm of the hands and this will reduce the much needed wrist action required in the swing. Conversely the grip that is too thin will allow the club to be gripped too much in the fingers and the wrist action will be excessive. As overactive wrists often cause 'hooking' and lack of wrist work – 'slicing' – you can see just how important grip thickness can be. The size of the player's hand is the guide to the correct thickness and the professional will know exactly how to advise you.

Grips are made of two basic materials, leather and rubber. Which you choose is a matter of personal preference, although as leather has become very expensive the rubber grip is much more common and considerably easier to maintain. If they become a little shiny or slippery, rubber grips can be given a good scrub with a nailbrush and soapy water. This will remove the dirt and perspiration that everyday play will cause to accumulate on the grip, and the little brown cork specks visible in the rubber absorb the soap, giving the grip a nice tacky feel. If this treatment does not have much effect, then it is probably time to have some new grips fitted and again a club professional is there to help. It only takes a little while, so little or no inconvenience is caused to the player. Holding on to a new grip is like gripping a new golf club.

It is very important to look after your equipment. The wooden clubs should always be dried, as the wood is prone to swelling if left wet and gaps will form around the insert (the plastic piece in the middle of the club face). Head covers, too, should always be dried after play. Shafts should always be dried as they can rust, particularly where the head and shaft join.

Often golf clubs are put in the car boot after play on a Sunday and then not looked at again until the following Saturday morning. Look after your clubs and they will look after you. Grips and shoe spikes should be well maintained. The professional is the man to look after all your needs, from new grips or refitting the binding round the wooden club neck, to refurbishing your favourite wood. By the time he has finished your club can look like new.

Golf balls should always be of reasonable quality, as badly scuffed or cut ones can adversely affect the way the ball flies. The best ball for the beginner to buy is the two-piece or so-called 'solid' ball. It is more difficult to cut or mark than the other makes and definitely goes further.

RULE BOOK

The maximum number of clubs you may carry is fourteen.
If you are unfortunate enough to break a club, you may replace it.
If a ball becomes unfit for play it may be replaced subject to your opponent's agreement. A ball falling off a tee-peg is replaced even if it is knocked off by the player himself.

Introducing the Swing

As golf is played with a stationary ball, the preparation to strike that ball is extremely important. Most of the swinging movements are determined by the manner in which you stand or set-up to the ball. It is important to analyse the elements of that set-up and discipline yourself into performing them in a definite and consistent routine. As most faults in golf are caused by an incorrect set-up, you must try to get the static positions correct. This should not be too difficult, even for the beginner.

The aim of this set-up is to try to pre-set your body in the impact or hitting position, before you move a muscle in the swing.

The Sequence

1. Aim – the club aimed at the target.
2. Grip – the hold on the club.
3. Ball position – relative to the player's feet.
4. Stance and body alignment.
5. Posture.

Once these five positions have been achieved, and in the order laid down, you are ready to consider the swing. The player should remember this order, so that none of the stages is missed out as this will cause confusion. Even the tournament professional will follow this sequence religiously, so if it's good enough for him it must be for the rest of us. Now let's look at each in detail.

Aim

It may seem very obvious that the club should be aimed at the target but many teaching professionals will point out that it is often neglected.

The front of the club face is called the leading edge. This is placed at right-angles to the intended line of flight with the sole, or bottom of the club, resting on the ground. The club is now lying correctly for itself and aimed in the proper direction.

It is important that you check the blade regularly throughout the routine, as the slightest change can greatly effect the overall result.

The club face is the only part that points to the hole. Everything else is parallel to the ball to target line.

Grip

The grip or hold on the club is by far the most important stage that the beginner has to learn to be a successful player. It is still as true today as when it was first stated, that there has never been a good player with a bad grip or vice versa, and although there are no guarantees in golf, a good grip is as close as you will get to one. The trouble with learning the grip is that it is the most boring part. Most beginners feel that they only have to grab hold of the club and give the ball a good thrash. However, as any experienced player will tell you, the grip is the basis of each part of the swing. As his hands are the only part of the player to touch the club, it is the grip that controls the angle of the club blade throughout the swing, and after all the ball will only do what the club face tells it to.

It is essential to consider how to assemble the hold on the club and the reasons for each step. The basic principle is to play a backhanded shot with the left hand and a forehanded shot with the right hand. If you stand with your arms hanging freely at one side you will see that your hands do hang naturally in this position.

The overlapping or Vardon grip

With the fingers of your left hand pointing at the ground, place the club through the middle joint of your index finger. It passes diagonally across your palm to a point at the bottom of the callous pad, or half an inch from the end of your little finger. Close your hand on to the handle (Do not wrap it around as this will re-align your forearm and cause problems at a later stage), until, depending on the size of your hand, 2 – 3 knuckles are visible on the back of your left hand.

Now place your thumb to the right of centre of the handle. This will support the weight of the club at the top of the back swing. You arrive at this position with your thumb directly underneath the shaft. The main pressure, although reasonably light, is mostly in your last three fingers.

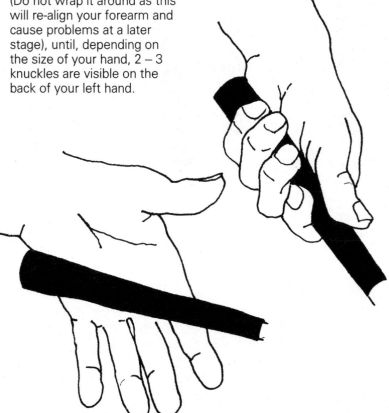

On your right hand, again
with fingers pointing at the
ground, place the handle
through the middle joint of
the index finger. Pass the
club across your hand, going
through the end of your little
finger. Your hand closes
around the handle. Your right
index finger is now crooked
in such a way as to provide a
cradle for the club to rest in
and your thumb should be
placed as comfortably as
possible, on the left side of
the handle.

The little finger of
your right hand is placed in
the groove between the
index and third fingers of
your left hand.

This encourages your hands
to work together, the little
finger acting as a claw to
bind your hands. It also has
the effect of reducing a little
of the strength on your right
hand and makes it easier to
have equality between the
hands. The pressure on your
right hand is in the middle
two fingers.

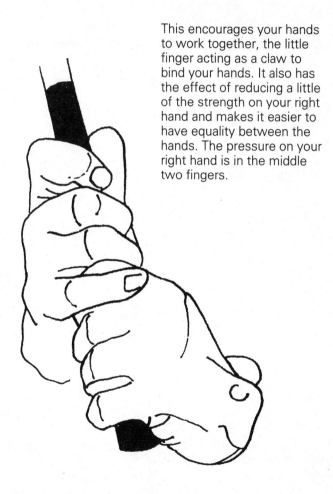

When both hands are placed correctly on the club, the palms should be facing each other and the 'V' shape formed between the index finger and thumb on both hands will point between your chin and your right shoulder. Your hands have now been married and will work as a team.

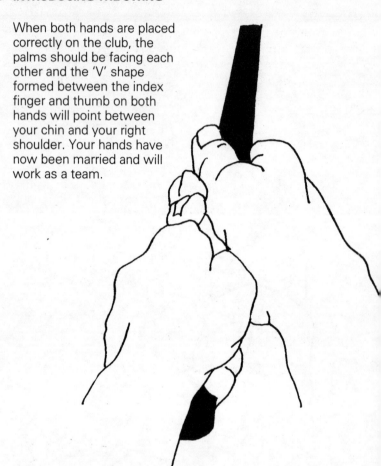

Holding the club in the fingers of the right hand provides a real sense of feel. If the club is held in the palm of the right hand all the mobility of the right wrist is lost, causing a reduction of power. A good way to demonstrate this feel is to write your name with a pen, holding it in your fingers, this allows your hand and wrist to flow freely. Now hold the pen in the palm of your hand and you will notice how jerky and uncontrollable an action this becomes.

An alternative to the overlapping or Vardon grip, is the interlocking grip. While there is nothing new in this grip, players such as Jack Nicklaus have brought it back into vogue and it has become popular with younger players. When used with the guidelines already laid down, this grip is perfectly acceptable.

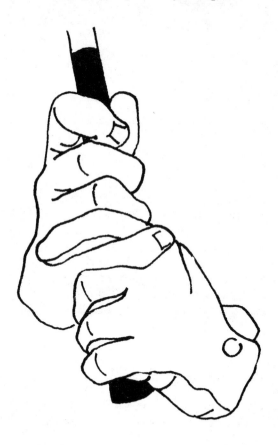

The interlocking grip is where the little finger of the right hand and the forefinger of the left hand intertwine.

FAULT-FINDER

Sadly many players interpret the interlocking part as the most important piece of the interlocking grip. By interlocking first, the club is held too much in the palm, causing the loss of flexibility already described, and also loss of feel.

The third variation on the grip is the ten finger, or baseball grip, where all fingers are placed on the club. This is supposedly suitable for players with smaller hands. This grip is best ignored, as the hands are totally separated and will work independently. If your hands are on the smaller side then the professional can fit thinner grips and you can get over the problem that way. Although I recommend the Vardon grip, the beginner can try both this and the interlocking grip and settle on whichever works the better for him.

While no one will pretend that the grip will feel comfortable at this early stage – stick with it, it's the best golfing friend you can have. Although there have been incredible changes in equipment and golf swing theories over the years, the Vardon grip has been around since the early 1900's so it has proved itself.

Ball position

The hitting zone is from the middle of the stance forward, and that's where you should have the ball. The longer the club, the further forward the ball is positioned. For the wooden clubs the ball will be positioned opposite your left heel and you will move progressively back, approximately 1″ per club, until you reach the centre of the stance.

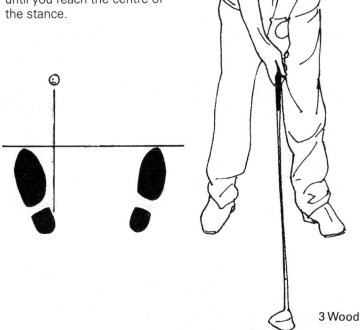

3 Wood

During the swing the club head is at its lowest point, just past the centre of the feet, so the driver is positioned in line with the left heel to catch the ball marginally on its upswing. This will cut down the

FAULT-FINDER
If at any time you go further back than centre,the attack on the ball would be too steep, resulting in a loss of power and great holes in the ground.

4 Iron

backspin and allow the ball to roll further and as distance is the name of the game with the wooden clubs, this is desirable. On the shorter irons you should play the ball at the centre of the feet, so that you can catch the ball on the downward swing. This will encourage backspin and make the ball stop more quickly on hitting the green.

Another school of thought on ball position suggests

Regardless of the system used, your hands are always opposite the inside of your left leg. This will mean that even with a driver, your hands will be level with the ball. This is important as if your hands were behind the ball, a wristy or flicking action would follow. When the right passes the left hand all power has been used.

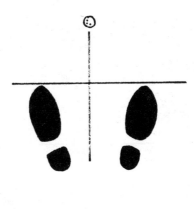

8 Iron

playing every club with the ball in line with your left heel, and widening your right foot as the clubs get longer. The idea behind this system is that the fewer changes one makes, the easier it is to be consistent. However this forward ball position makes it more difficult to keep your shoulders in line with the target, particularly with the shorter clubs, ie. eight, nine and wedge.

Width of stance

The widest part of anyone's body is the width across their shoulders, therefore a base is needed to support them. Your feet must be approximately shoulder-width apart. As the shaft of the club gets shorter, so the stance becomes slightly narrower. As the shorter swing is not so full, and therefore not quite so physical, the narrower stance will suffice. Your feet are placed just as you would walk, with the weight evenly distributed.

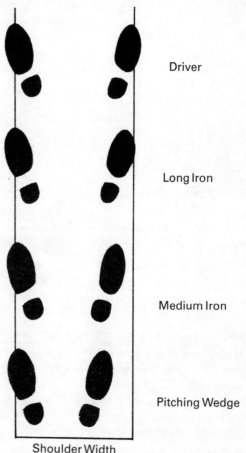

Driver

Long Iron

Medium Iron

Pitching Wedge

Shoulder Width

Stance and body alignment

Now that the club face is in line, you need to position your body so that it points in the same direction. This too, is essential to avoid arguments between the player and his club.

Your feet, hips and shoulders should be in line, parallel to an imaginary line drawn from the ball to the target. The popular analogy is that of standing on a railway track with the club head on one rail and the feet on the other.

When checking the line of your feet and shoulders they will not actually point at the target, but just to the left of it, although still parallel to the target line.

Again it is advisable to adopt a routine when trying to achieve good line-up.

The square stance

The leading edge of the blade should be introduced to the ball, at the same time bringing your right foot into position. This allows you to gauge the correct distance to stand from the ball, having first placed the sole of the club flat on the ground and made yourself feel comfortable. It also allows you to refer to the target without having to look past the left side.

Your left foot is then brought into position, level with your right toe. This makes you very aware of bringing your shoulders into line as well.

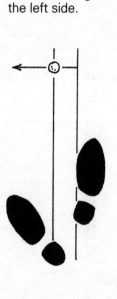

By following this routine it makes it virtually impossible for you to stand closed, ie. aiming to the right, as it is highly unlikely that you will ever allow your left foot to advance beyond your right. For a particularly good example of the square stance routine, watch the 1987 Open Champion, Nick Faldo. As the line of the shoulders controls the direction that the club is swung on, it is to be highly recommended and as in all swings, the preparation is vital.

FAULT-FINDER

1. Is the blade of the club pointing at the target?
2. Are your feet, hips and shoulders parallel to the line of the target?
3. Are your feet a comfortable distance apart, approximately shoulder-width, with the weight distribution 50/50?

When practising it is beneficial to have a club on the grass, midway between your feet and the ball, parallel to both, as this will confirm your aim and allow you to get the feel of it.

Posture

This has been a most neglected area in golf over the years. Without good posture it is impossible to have good balance throughout the swing and if there is any loss of balance there will be total loss of control. Good balance comes from the poise of the player in the set-up. It can only be achieved in one way.

Stand as tall as you can, using your full height, with your arms hanging freely in front of you. Bend forward from the hips until the club head just reaches the ground. The amount of bend will vary from club to club, depending on the length of the shaft. However, the spinal angle is still as nature intended and not curved. Your body weight is brought forward automatically, towards the balls of your feet.

You will feel the back of your knees tightening, since as one part of the body goes forward, another part automatically goes back. To take this pressure off your legs and spine, the knee position is softened. The knees do not bend. Hold your head clear of your chest to give a feeling of holding your body up, and turn your head slightly to the right.

This will encourage a full body turn during the swing. Do not overdo it as this will cause your left shoulder to drop at the start of the back swing and also cause loss of body height.

If this routine is done in reverse and your legs are positioned first, it creates a feeling of sitting down and your body weight will be back towards your heels.

A good player, who may be experiencing difficulty with his posture and overall set-up, can in fact find the correct position by making a slow swing and freezing at the point he would consider the perfect impact position. By posing in this position he can then remove the momentum from his legs and place the club head behind the ball on the grass. If this is the position, he knows he would like to adopt on impact, he can start off from here. After all it must be easier to return to a position than have to compromise and find another.

This completes the five points that go into making the set-up and you are now ready to build a golf swing. It is worth repeating at this stage that the good features in a swing are pre-determined by this good set-up.

FAULT-FINDER

Beware of the old golfing myth of sitting down on a coffee stool or shooting stick, it has long been discarded. Although regrettably it is still heard from time to time. Anything athletic has to be performed from the front end of the shoes and not the back. Only Scottish goalkeepers play off their heels.

Your head must never be kept down, another golfing myth, as this will cause restriction of the shoulder turn on the back swing and a very cramped follow-through.

The Swing

To hit a golf ball successfully, your whole body has to be committed to the swing. All the moving parts have but one thing in mind and that is to allow the club to swing and no matter which club, there is only one swing.

Let's consider the parts of your anatomy that combine to allow the swing to function as a free moving unit. The body can be divided into two areas: upper body from the waist up, to include the arms and shoulders and the lower body: hips, legs and feet. The swinging effect will come from your upper body and the real source of power from the lower. At this stage it is important to realise that the successful golf shot requires two things, direction and power. It really is that simple and if you work on the movements that will allow this to happen you will have a good understanding of how to move a club in the correct fashion and have a good chance of being consistent as well, something even the top tournament players desire.

RULE BOOK

If the ball moves when you address it, other than on the teeing ground, a penalty stroke is incurred. If a ball at rest is moved by another ball, then that ball will be replaced.

The 'waggle'

As a preliminary to the swing we have what is called the 'waggle'. This is purely and simply a gentle movement back and forth with the club head, hands and wrists, designed to ease the tension of the set-up and encourage a rhythmic start to the back swing.

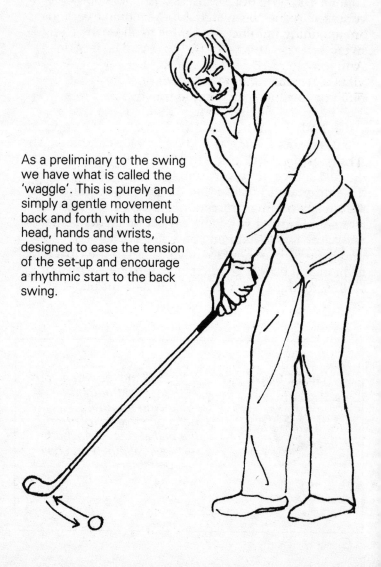

The half-swing

For the process of building a swing we start with the half-swing, that is taking the club back to waist level on both the back swing and follow-through.

Before moving the club there is a basic concept to consider. As has been stated earlier, the target line is an imaginary line that runs from the ball to the target. Everything to our side of the line is called 'inside'. Anything to the other side, or right of the target line as viewed from behind, is called 'outside' the line. To build the swing, start with the six iron.

The one-piece-takeaway

The first movement of the back swing or takeaway, is to move the club back along the target line, keeping it as low to the ground as possible for the first 12 inches (even further for the longer clubs).

By extending your left hand and arm back to waist level two things will happen: wherever your left hand and arm go, your left shoulder must follow and as your shoulder is introduced, the club will naturally swing inside the line.

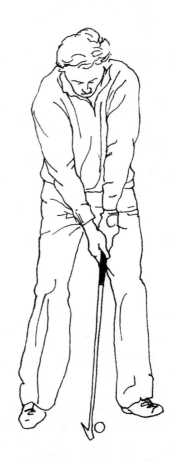

At waist level, the club face will now appear to point off to the right. However, in fact the club face is still square to the target and this can be checked in two ways. Firstly, the leading edge of the club face will still be at right-angles to your shoulders and the knuckles visible on the back of your left hand will still be the same as in the set-up.

Secondly, due to the extension back from the ball, you will feel the weight transferring to your right side. This is not a conscious, but responsive, action. Your right knee will have remained comfortably flexed as in the set-up. All parts of your body have been encouraged to work together.

The first 18" – 24" is probably the most important part of the golf swing. You have done your best to ensure that the club face remains square to the target but you can also see that the big muscles of your body, the shoulders and the legs, have been encouraged to become involved.

The forward swing commences with the lateral movement of your hips and legs. Your left heel, which will have cleared the ground on the back swing, (although only marginally as you only made a half swing) will then go back down on to the grass. There cannot be a lateral shift if your left heel remains off the ground. Your hands and arms will then swing through to waist level and your body weight will now be on the left shoe.

Already co-ordination between the club and the player has been created as both are moving in the same direction at the same time. During this half-swing no conscious effort should be made to hit the ball. You should feel that contact is made because the ball happens to be in the way of the path of the club head.

Once you have experienced this back and forward movement of the club and all the responsive actions you can progress to the fuller swing.

The full swing

C

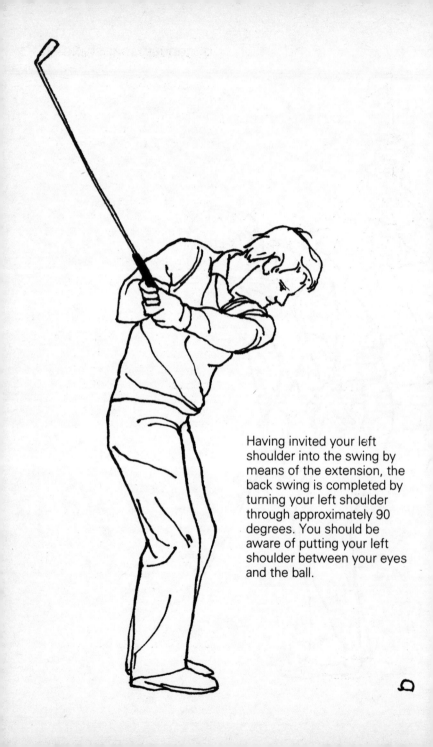

Having invited your left shoulder into the swing by means of the extension, the back swing is completed by turning your left shoulder through approximately 90 degrees. You should be aware of putting your left shoulder between your eyes and the ball.

Your body weight will transfer even further on to the right side and you will feel your whole body weight over your right hip, knee and ankle. As your hips will have turned through only 45 degrees there will be a feeling of tension around your hip muscles. This means that your upper body has been 'wound up' against your lower body and when this tension is released, you have created the ability to hit the ball powerfully.

At the top, your left arm should be comfortably straight or extended not held deliberately straight as this really is physically impossible, although it was advocated for many years.

The wrist action or wrist cock as it is called, that will occur on the back swing is taken care of by the weight of the golf club and the momentum of the swing. This wrist cock is never, never a conscious action. It will break the line of the swing if you try to perform it as a deliberate movement. At the top of the back swing, the line along the club shaft will again be parallel to the ball-to-target line.

At the top of the back swing you should feel that your body has been 'wound-up' or coiled like a spring and this provides the means with which to hit the ball. If it is possible to hold this position for any length of time then nothing has been created. When you relax this tension at speed, which will be instinctive, you release the spring.

The big muscles that we spoke about earlier are now totally committed. It is these big muscles that dictate the speed and rhythm of the swing, as they take longer to move than the little ones in the hands and the wrists. By being aware of moving the big muscles in your shoulders in the second half of the back swing, you prevent the swing from becoming too quick – a big problem when you experience pressure at a later stage when playing the game.

FAULT-FINDER

Are you allowing the small muscles to dominate? If so they overtake the larger ones and throw your timing completely.

You are now fully prepared to strike the ball and follow- through.

From the top of the back swing, the tension that you created will be released instinctively and your body weight can transfer completely into your left side.

As your left heel cleared the ground on the back swing, you created a space to move back into as your left heel returns to the ground.

FAULT-FINDER
Are you trying to 'release' your hands on the down swing? This will cause the radius of the swing to increase and the club head will enter the ground before the ball resulting in 'fat' or heavy shots. Again the little muscles will have too much to say and so destroy everything you have been working for.

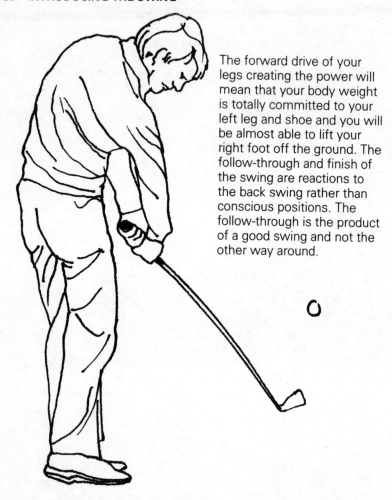

The forward drive of your legs creating the power will mean that your body weight is totally committed to your left leg and shoe and you will be almost able to lift your right foot off the ground. The follow-through and finish of the swing are reactions to the back swing rather than conscious positions. The follow-through is the product of a good swing and not the other way around.

The release that one continually hears and reads about, is not something the golfer really wants to concern himself with. It is a result of all the other correct swing movements. It is not a conscious move that you make with your hands as so many players seem to feel. As it is, it is a movement that happens after the ball has been struck and not before.

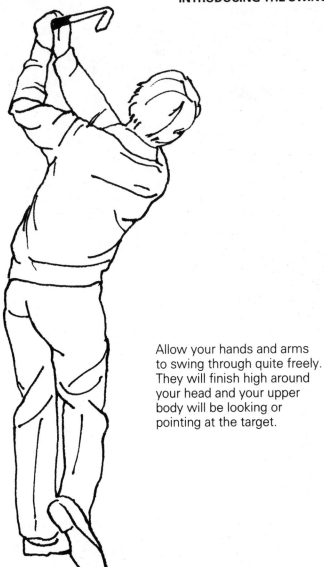

Allow your hands and arms to swing through quite freely. They will finish high around your head and your upper body will be looking or pointing at the target.

FAULT-FINDER

Is your back swing restricted, and your shoulder turn and follow-through cut short? This is because you are keeping your head down. Your weight will remain on your right foot, greatly reducing the power. Your head controls the balance of your body and by keeping it steady throughout most of the swing, you will give the swing a central point.

Remember the real power comes from your legs and not your hands but because they respond and are not conscious you feel that they are very quiet. Nothing could be further from the truth. The best analogy is that of a boxer throwing a punch. If he were to keep his feet flat on the ground, of course he could still hit his opponent but the punch wouldn't do a great deal of damage. However, if he allows his body weight to move in the same direction as his fist then all his movements are co-ordinated and his body weight backs-up his fist and power is created. For the golfer substitute club head for fist!

RULE BOOK

If you have to search for a ball the rules allow you five minutes to look for it but don't ask other people to wait for that five minutes.

At this stage it might be worth making a point about the head. How often does one hear "keep your head down". This is one of the golfing myths. The head should be held steady throughout the back swing and most of the follow-through. However as the momentum of the swing takes the club head through to approximately waist level, the golfer's head should be allowed to come up and see where the ball has gone. The problem with keeping your head down is that you will tend to bury your chin in your chest and clamp your head into a fixed position.

GOOD MANNERS

Courtesy demands that you should give your opponents the chance to do their best at all times. This means standing absolutely still, out of their peripheral vision and keeping quiet. (The best place to stand is opposite the person's face as they will know exactly where you are. If you stand behind the person they may feel that they could hit you with the club and directly behind in the line of the shot is very distracting). A breach of this unwritten rule is bad manners and could also be interpreted as gamesmanship.

As has been repeated throughout the pages of this book there is one swing for all the clubs. All the different shots that are required and the distances that have to be achieved are taken care of by the clubs themselves. However, the beginner may notice when watching other people playing the game, that the club appears to swing on different angles around the body. For example, the shorter irons may appear to be more upright than the longer irons and the wooden clubs. This is due entirely to the length of the shaft and the angle between the shaft and the ground.

The angle that the club travels around the body is referred to as 'swing plane'. Again this is something that the player himself need not worry about unduly. Although in terms of the golf swing it is extremely important, happily the plane is virtually self-finding. It is decided by the angle of the spine, which in turn is decided by the height of the player and the length of the club shaft.

The feeling when hitting with a wooden club is of a sweeping action, while the iron clubs, because of the divot taken – slight with the long and medium irons and bigger with the shorter irons – is more of a punching action. This is not a conscious act on behalf of the player but as a result of the ball position and the other factors we have discussed.

As you stand closer for the shorter clubs, the spinal angle will be more severe, therefore the swing will be more upright.

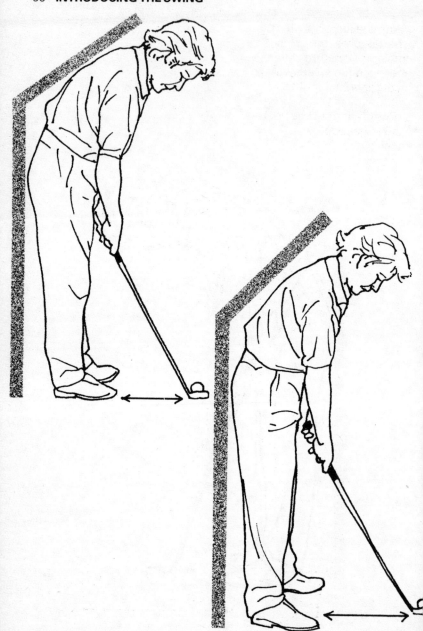

With the longer shaft, the straighter spine will mean the shoulder turn is flattened. So while you may feel the swing slightly differently initially, the basic movement from the upper and lower body is unchanged.

The Short Game

You have now arrived close to the green and even the
full wedge shot (the shortest iron) will still hit the
ball too far. Your aim is to restrict the distance the ball
will travel and yet still hit it in a positive manner. So
often I see golfers trying to hit the ball softly. This
usually means the club decelerates into the ball and
only sends it a few yards. "Head up" everyone cries –
it's nothing to do with that at all. The player has just
not been positive in his action through the ball.

When you play the little shots, the basic distance is
controlled by the length of the back swing.

The Follow-Through

The follow-through is designed to show the ball where you want it to go.

Try throwing a ball under-arm, to prove this theory to yourself. Start with a gentle action on the first ball and on the second ball, try to throw it further. As you can feel it's the back swing that you have increased. On that first throw did your hand stop the minute you let the ball go? No, your hand followed on to indicate to the ball where the target was and therefore where the ball was supposed to go. Pitching as we call this restrictive shot is exactly the same.

Now you need some help to vary the distance by controlling the back swing. The width of stance contributes to the power, so the first thing to do is narrow that stance, but by how much?

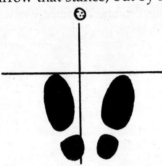

Start by restricting the stance almost entirely and place your feet a couple of inches apart. This will restrict the length of the back swing totally. Now, holding the club in the normal way, make a few comfortable swings at the ball (as much as the narrow stance will allow) and see how far the balls go.

You will find they group together quite nicely and this distance will give you a base figure from which to operate. Once you have decided what this distance is, by pacing out to the middle of the pile of golf balls, you can then make the stance progressively wider. This will allow you the freedom to increase the length of the back swing and so make the ball travel a little further.

Once you arrive at the full width of stance you will be at the maximum distance for your wedge. With practice you will be able to gauge how wide a stance you need for certain distances. In my experience, with hands at the top of the handle, and feet a couple of inches apart, most players can manage between twenty five and thirty yards. This is the base figure on which we operate.

You now know how to make the ball go further than this distance, (the 25-30 yard or base figure), and up to a full shot, but what if you need it shorter than that? How can you restrict your swing even further? Your hands will move down the handle of the club.

The shorter club has less leverage and so the back swing is shortened even further. Again with practice, you will be able to assess just how far you have to go

---

FAULT-FINDER

Do you try to lift the ball into the air, particularly if there is an obstacle in the way? If you allow the loft on the club to take care of the manner in which the ball will behave, and as the follow-through is designed to make the ball go to the target, you can literally follow through as far as you like without effecting the distance the ball will travel.

down the handle. However, do not move your hands down the handle until your feet are nearly together. If you do, one move is only compromising the other, and you are making two changes to the original set-up when one will do. As with all golf shots, the wrist cock depends on the length of the swing and the momentum. It will occur naturally, so it really is one less thing to have to think about.

You have now got even closer to the green and cannot restrict your set-up any further. Judging the distance to the flag now is really a matter of hand/eye co-ordination and practice. However you can still apply one or two rules to make life as easy as possible.

If the grass around the edge of the green, or the fringe as it is called, is fairly short then it is possible to putt the ball, which is the easiest way to play the shot. As keeping the ball close to the ground is the safest shot of all. The chip is used when a putt is not possible.

The chip
The chip shot can be played with a variety of clubs and circumstance should always dictate which club is used. By practising, a player can work out the ratio of length of time the ball will spend in the air to the amount of roll he can expect, for each club. For example the seven iron will carry the ball through 25% of the overall distance in the air and run 75 %, a nine iron carries 50% and then runs 50%, the wedge will carry 75% and then run 25%. This is only an approximation and you will have to work out your own ratios.

Always remember that the more time the ball spends on the ground, the easier it is to judge distance.

Let me explain this further and you can even prove it to yourself. Taking a putter, give the ball sufficient strength to make it go 10 yards. Now play the shot with a seven iron and give it the same amount of strength. The ball will probably only travel about 7 or 8 yards. Why? because some of the energy is used to send the ball into the air. Now with the wedge and the tremendous amount of loft on the club, 10 yards worth of strength will probably only send the ball 5 or 6 yards, as most of it will send the ball into the air. A simple test you might think, but as you can see it proves conclusively that to get 10 yards of distance out of a wedge, you may have to hit the ball considerably harder than you may at first have thought. There are some top professionals who will play all their chip shots with one club, but the average player will find it much easier to follow this advice and keep the ball close to the ground.

The less loft on the club, the less time the ball spends in the air and the further the ball will run.

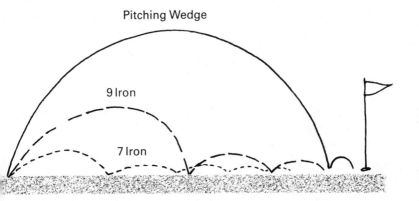

The technique

When playing the chip shot, as always the normal grip is taken.

Always try to visualise the shot in your mind before executing it. A mental picture will help in choosing the correct club for the job.

The ball is played closer to your right foot and your hands will therefore be a little further forward of the ball than normal. This shot is played exclusively with your hands and arms. You are trying to eliminate as many of the moving parts as possible and retain the relationship between the club and the hands and arms throughout the stroke.

There is definitely no wrist action in chipping. Any suggestion of it will cause a flicking action, which can catch the ball thinly or the wrist work can increase the back spin on the ball. This makes it very difficult to assess the amount of roll achieved for the club being used.

The club is swung straight back and straight through, along the target line. It is moved at an even pace to keep it under control. As with the pitching technique it is the length of the back swing that controls the distance and the follow-through is the guiding arm, so don't be afraid to follow through. Stopping at the ball, or decelerating causes more fluffed chips than even 'head up'.

FAULT-FINDER
Are you are experiencing too much back-spin on the ball? Check that there is no flick of the wrist in your action.

Putting

When it comes to creating a score in golf, putting plays the most significant part. If you play well and putt badly you will have a fairly ordinary score, on the other hand if you putt well and hit the ball poorly, you can still get the ball around the course in a reasonable number. Putting does represent half of the strokes in the par score on the golf course, so if you can excel at it, you can be a useful competitor. When you watch the top tournament professionals, each appears to putt in a different style. The fundamentals still apply however and we will follow the usual sequence here as we examine them.

Aim
The club face is aimed in the usual way with the leading edge at right-angles to the hole.

Grip
There are several significant changes to the grip when putting. As the shaft of the putter is nearly perpendicular, the handle passes more through your palm than in the conventional grip.

All the modern day putters are fitted with a grip that is flat on the top. This will encourage you to place your thumbs correctly and your hands will point at the target.

The most significant change is to have both thumbs down the front of the handle. The little finger can be overlapped or interlocked in the usual way, again whichever is the most comfortable.

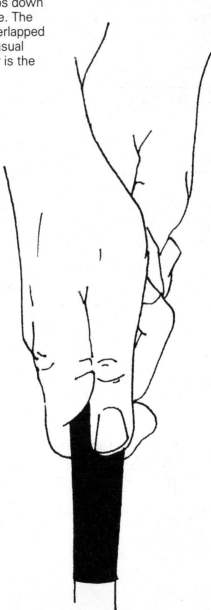

The 'Reverse Overlap'

This is another way of placing the hands together for putting and it is highly favoured by the tournament professional.

It is designed to firm up the left wrist and therefore stop the right hand from passing the left, which would ruin the blade alignment.

The forefinger of your left hand passes over the fingers of your right hand.

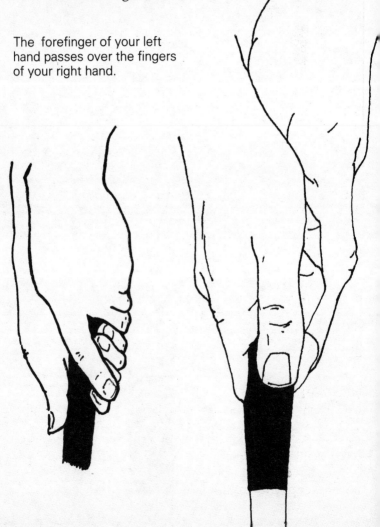

GOOD MANNERS

The green-staff at golf clubs put a lot of effort into providing us with good putting surfaces. We should all do our best to assist them by ALWAYS repairing our pitch marks; (that is the indentation made in the grass by the ball on a full shot). A pitchfork can be bought from any Professional's shop and this should be as important a part of your equipment as a putter. Try to develop a habit of repairing your own and one other pitchmark on every green and that will soon eliminate the problem.

The only advice here is to give each one a try and settle on the one that works best for you. The old story in putting is that if it works, it's correct. The grip pressure should be really quite light, as this will improve the feel and also encourage smoothness in the stroke.

Ball position
Ideally the ball should be set just inside your left foot. There are two reasons for this. Firstly, it will encourage the putter head to hit the ball slightly on the upswing which will give a smoother roll on the ball, as it will encourage overspin. Secondly, it ensures that the putter keeps moving on line towards the hole.

Stance and body alignment

Width of stance is unimportant provided it feels comfortable. It doesn't really matter how a golfer sets himself to putt so long as he considers two factors.

The stance must allow you to be balanced, if not the stroke will be jerky. The stance must allow your head and body to remain motionless throughout the movement. However, until you gain more experience it would be best to aim in the usual way, with your body parallel to the target line.

Posture

As your body is not involved in putting, posture is not all that important, other than to try to keep your eyes over the ball. This will encourage the putter head to swing on line throughout the stroke.

To check this, stand over the ball and hold a second ball in your right hand, level with your eyes. Drop the ball to the ground and if your eyes are level, it should land on top of the ball on the grass. Once again, personal comfort is the most important factor. Raymond Floyd stands very tall to the ball and he uses an extra long putter. Jack Nicklaus on the other hand, crouches over the ball and as both are extremely fine putters, you can see there are no cast iron rules. Select which is the best posture for you, by experimentation.

During the stroke, try to make sure that the back swing and the through swing follow along the target line at a constant pace. The putter head should be kept low to the ground, as this will encourage it to swing on line.

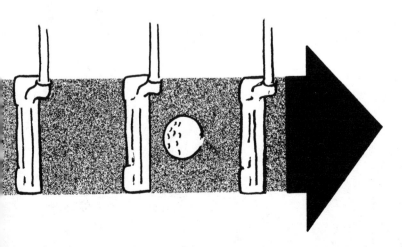

The swing on the putting stroke is very pendulum-like and therefore the length of the follow-through should at least equal that of the back swing.

As with chipping, the length of the back swing determines the distance, and the follow-through, the direction. By trying to maintain a constant pace on the stroke it is much easier to maintain control.

FAULT-FINDER

Do you find it difficult to control the roll of the ball? You are probably accelerating the putter head through the ball. The putt is being hit as opposed to stroked and it is extremely difficult to control the path of the putter head and the roll on the ball.

As the putt gets longer, so the stance should widen, so that even with the longer, pendulum-type stroke, your body can still be kept very still.

As with all the touch shots, practice is to be recommended. Develop a set routine of setting-up to the putt and always have a practice swing, trying to duplicate the length of stroke that will be needed on the putt you are about to attempt.

Unfortunately, not all putting greens are flat, so you have one further consideration. You have to learn to 'read' the green and assess the breaks. You can best do this by lining up the putt from directly behind the ball. You then have to calculate just how much to aim off on the high side of the hole, to allow the slope to take its effect. Once you have selected your aiming point, treat each putt as a straight one to that spot and produce your normal stroke to that new target and not the hole.

Other features that have to be taken into account will be the uphill putt which will require a firmer stroke and the downhill, which will require a shorter one. Again the slopes can be taken into account from behind the ball, or even as you approach the green.

Wet greens too have to be allowed for, since the ball will not turn so quickly and it will be travelling more slowly on the damp surface. With all these factors to be taken into account, always take time when assessing your putt.

On the longer putts, pace is all important and it is enough to try and get the ball within 18" to 2ft of the hole, leaving a relatively simple putt for the second one.

FAULT-FINDER

Do you find the ball invariably misses and lands to the left of the hole on shorter putts, from 2-3 feet? It could be that you are looking for the ball falling into the hole. Listen, rather than look, as head movement can be very destructive and will cause the ball to miss, invariably finishing on the left of the hole.

Bunker Play

There are two types of bunker shot that we have to learn to play. The greenside bunker and the fairway bunker.

The Greenside Bunker

This is the only swing that varies in the whole of golf. For the first time you really don't want to send the ball forward, you are more concerned with getting it up over the lip or bank of the bunker. However, you do have to hit the ball positively to achieve this, therefore certain changes have to be made.

This is the out-to-in swing often referred to in bunker shots. It is not a conscious effort to swing in this fashion, it is taken care of by the alignment. Since your

The out-to-in swing

The blade of the club is aimed, as usual, at the target and the club is gripped in the normal fashion. However as in all hazards, you are not allowed to touch the ground.

The ball is positioned in line with your left heel. Your body alignment should be well to the left of the target. This is referred to as 'standing open'.

At this point in the stance, wriggle your feet into the sand. This gives you a firm foundation in the sand and removes the possibility of slipping. It also tests the surface of the sand to give an indication as to how hard you may have to swing.

Lowering your body position will automatically lower the bottom of the swing and encourage the club head to go down underneath the ball. As the club face and your body are not pointing in the same direction, you will create a slight conflict between the two. Swing the club along the line of your feet and shoulders, cutting across the target line.

The ball's direction is controlled by the aim of the club face.

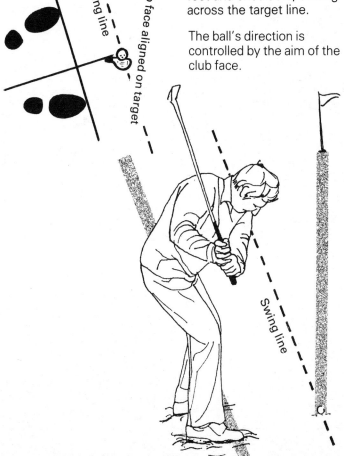

shoulders do not turn as much as in the full shot, the wrist action will be much greater and so the attack on the ball will be much steeper and encourage the extra height. To weaken the power in the shot, you should try to make the club enter the sand approximately 1" behind the ball. This layer or cushion of sand between the blade of the club and the ball will diffuse the power.

Once you have the confidence to swing through to the target quite freely and realise that the ball will be going up rather than forward, you can alter the distance the ball will travel by varying the speed of the swing.

RULE BOOK

In a bunker, the club must not be grounded in the set-up.

Provisional ball: is played for a ball that may be lost outside a water hazard or may be out of hands.

Lost ball: A player is allowed to search for five minutes then he must return to where that shot was played if the original ball is not found and two penalty strokes added to his score. The ball will always be played as it lies unless special club rules are in force.

A ball can be marked lifted and cleaned on the green before putting.

The sand iron
In time the beginner may add a sand iron to his set of clubs. This is a specialist club for the sand shot.

If you look at the sole of this iron, it differs dramatically from all the others. On the iron clubs, numbered one through wedge, the leading edge of the sole is higher than the back edge. This is to allow the player to take a divot underneath the ball, imparting back spin on the stroke. The sand iron is the reverse.

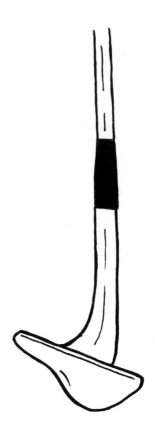

It allows the leading edge to penetrate the soft powdery sand and the back edge of the sole bounces or skids off the sand. This will mean that the depth of the sand taken is controlled by the club, so the player does not have to dig down on the ball and explode the ball out on to the green.

This type of bunker shot is called the 'splash' shot, and as the word conveys, only a light layer of sand is removed from under the ball.

FAULT-FINDER

Never try to force the ball out of the bunker as this will encourage the ball to be hit in a forward direction – not the desired effect at all.

Sometimes in the greenside bunker, the ball stays in its own impression. This is called a 'plugged' ball and an adjustment to the technique has to be applied. All you are trying to do in this situation is to get the ball out on to the green.

Square up your stance and position the ball very close to your right shoe. Place more weight on your left shoe to encourage what will be virtually a straight up and down swinging action. Still aim to hit 1" behind the ball, but on the downswing really accelerate your hands and club head.

The club will dig deeply down into the sand and there will be little or no follow-through, as the amount of sand will offer a great restriction to the through swing. The ball will pop up into the air and will not have very much back spin on it, so you must allow for the ball to roll.

All you are trying to do here is get 'out of jail' so don't worry if you don't get too close the flag.

Fairway Bunkers

Firstly, select a club with sufficient loft to clear the bank of the bunker. The golden rule in the fairway bunker is not to be greedy. If you think you can get out with the six iron, use the eight iron for safety. You will have to make a couple of adjustments to catch the ball cleanly during the swing.

The aim of the club is square to the target and the position of your hands on the club is as normal. However, the club is held a bit tighter and also a little further down the handle.

The firmer grip will help to eliminate some of the wrist action and reduce the possibility of 'fluffing' the ball. You have gone down the handle, to compensate for your feet being a little lower than the ball. (The wriggling of the feet is only slight, compared to the greenside shot, as you don't want to go into the sand nearly so deeply, just establish a firm base).

The ball should be positioned opposite the centre of your feet, to reduce the risk of catching the sand before the ball, causing a weak strike. The alignment is square to the target. To further encourage a clean contact

with the ball, concentrate on the top of the ball. The normal swing is then employed.

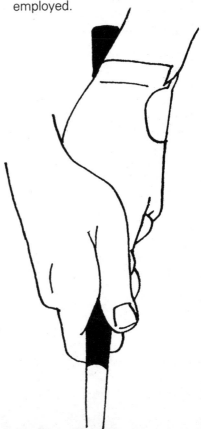

Awkward Lies

Unfortunately, golf courses are not flat so you have to be able to respond to the challenges presented by the course. There are four main types of awkward lie for which you must be prepared. These are up hill, down hill, ball above your feet and ball below your feet.

The Uphill Lie

Most players find this the easiest of the awkward lies, as the upward slope helps to get the ball airborne. You have to take extra club for the distance required, as the ball will fly higher than normal. This means that if a six would normally carry the ball the distance required, you will have to take a five iron or even more, depending on the severity of the slope.

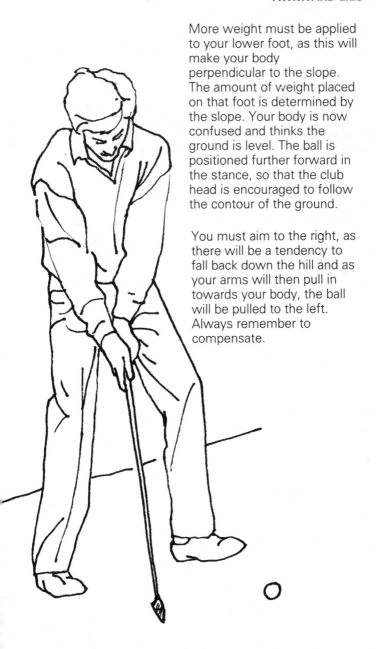

More weight must be applied to your lower foot, as this will make your body perpendicular to the slope. The amount of weight placed on that foot is determined by the slope. Your body is now confused and thinks the ground is level. The ball is positioned further forward in the stance, so that the club head is encouraged to follow the contour of the ground.

You must aim to the right, as there will be a tendency to fall back down the hill and as your arms will then pull in towards your body, the ball will be pulled to the left. Always remember to compensate.

The Down Hill Lie

This is the most difficult of the sloping lies as the ground is higher than the ball. The great tendency is to hit the grass before the ball, resulting in a weak or 'fluffed' shot. Take less club, ie. a six iron instead of a five iron.

Angle your body with the slope and allow your lower foot to bear your weight. (On the up hill and down hill lies always remember the weight is positioned in the lower shoe). If you try to remember left for down and right for up, then should you get one wrong, you will get them both wrong. The ball is positioned near your right foot, as you want to make the club head follow the slope after the ball has been struck.

This has the effect of de-lofting the club face, so the ball will travel further as it is going lower. As you have placed more weight in the left shoe to avoid catching the ground before the ball, this weight distribution will make the swing more upright. As a result there will be a tendency for the ball to drift to the right in flight. This should be allowed for in the set-up, by aiming off to the left.

Ball Below your Feet

In this situation, the natural tendency is to place your weight in your heels, as this will stop your body from falling forward during the shot. Unfortunately, this upright posture would cause a flatter swing and make it impossible for you to get down to the ball. Therefore you must go against this natural tendency and lean down the slope, since the more upright swing this creates allows a more descending attack on the ball.

As this type of swing will restrict your shoulder turn, the power will be reduced and the ball will have a tendency to go to the right. Again allowance should be made for this in the alignment. The ball should be placed in the centre of the feet.

Ball Above your Feet

Once again, resist the tendency to lean into the slope. Your weight should be placed towards the back of the shoes. This will help to flatten the swing and make it easier to strike the ball cleanly off the slope. Any suggestion of an upright swing, caused by leaning into the slope, would result in a digging action and the club would make contact with the ground too soon. The flatter swing will encourage your shoulders to turn. So on this shot you can expect to achieve good distance.

The objective in playing the sloping lies is to let yourself swing as normally as possible, by positioning your body as perpendicular to the slope as possible. By following this simple rule, you reduce the tendency of catching the ground before the ball on the uphill lie and topping or thinning on the downhill lie.

FAULT-FINDER

Do you often hook this shot? Then you are probably not allowing for the fact that the flatter plane will cause the ball to travel from right to left (a hook), so you should aim to the right of the target to allow for this.

There is quite a lot to remember on all these awkward lies, but if you can programme a golfing computer in your mind, before the swing is made, then coupled with practice, the fear can be removed. You can work on a positive approach and not worry about what might go wrong.

GOOD MANNERS

Remember to put your divots back. Players seem oblivious to the great holes they leave in the fairways and it seems unfair that because of someone's thoughtlessness, a bad lie can be achieved on the fairway after a good tee shot.

Bunkers too, should always be smoothed out after a shot has been played. There is nothing worse than landing in someone's heel print just because they have failed to clean up their mess.

Recovery Shots

As the heading, suggests you have hit the ball into
trouble. Rule one is to get the ball back into play as
quickly as possible and accept the fact that you are
likely to drop a stroke to par. Most golfers are a little
greedy and attempt shots that even the greatest player
would not contemplate. These miracle shots have two
chances – slim and none at all. Once again, try to cut
your losses and get back on to the fairway. Thick
rough is usually the biggest problem. As usual stick to
the formula laid down when building a swing.

This angle of attack will automatically de-loft the club,
so it is essential that you use one with plenty of loft.

GOOD MANNERS

Slow play has become a
real bug-bear over the last
few years and yet just by
using some commonsense
it doesn't take a lot to
speed up. No one ever
objects to the length of
time a player takes to play
his shot, weighing up all
the possibilities, but there
is no need to waste time.

The normal grip is quite suitable to allow you to escape from even the worst lie. Do not tighten your grip, as this will result in a loss of mobility in your wrist and actually reduce the strength. The ball will be positioned further back in the stance between the centre and the right foot.

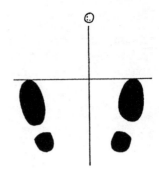

This will allow the club head a downward attack on the ball and so a cleaner contact will be made. It reduces the chances of catching the grass before the ball and that grass would offer resistance to the club head and reduce power.

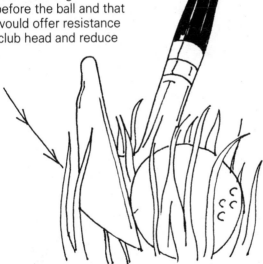

Another factor to consider in playing out of the rough is the direction of the growth of the grass. If the grass is growing against the direction of the shot, it will resist and tend to close the club face. You will then have to aim to the right.

If on the other hand, the grass should be growing in the same direction as the intended direction of the ball, it will be much easier to get through. There will still, however, be some grass between the ball and the club face and this reduces the back spin, as the grooves on the club will not be given the chance to do their job. Therefore you should take less club, since the ball will have a considerable amount of roll.

This shot is referred to as a 'flyer', as you get more

The high shot

To hit the high shot, simply play the ball forward in your stance, with hands slightly behind the ball. This will increase the loft on the club and allow the ball to be struck with the club face on the upswing.

distance out of the club than you could normally expect. If the rough grass is really thick, a simple pitch back on to the fairway is the sensible approach. It might well have to be 'brute force and ignorance'.

Another situation might arise in which you are required to hit the ball higher than normal, over a bush or a tree for example. Alternatively, you may have to hit the ball lower than normal, to negotiate the overhanging branches of some trees.

The low shot

To make the ball fly low, position the ball back in the stance and keep your hands well ahead of the ball. Place a little more weight in the left shoe. By keeping the weight in the left shoe during the swing, body movement will be greatly reduced and it will become more of a hand and arm swing.

On the downward swing, hit quite hard with your hands and arms and once again, the follow-through will be restricted because of the lack of body movement. This will allow the ball to be driven forward and keep it under the obstacle.

Playing on the Course

Playing the Game

The course is made up of eighteen holes and each one is a par 3, 4 or 5. Par is dependent on the distance of the hole and is the score the scratch golfer is supposed to score. You are allocated two putts on every green and expected to reach the par 3 in one full shot, the 4's in two shots and the par 5 in three strokes.

The distances
(MEN)
Par three – 250 yards and under
Par four – 251 yards to 475 yards
Par five – 476 yard and over

(LADIES)
Par three – 200 yards and under
Par four – 201 yard to 400 yards
Par five – 401 yards and over

The normal breakdown on the average golf course will be 4 par 3's, 10 par 4's and 4 par 5's, giving a total of 72. This score is then the basis for the handicapping system which we will look at in depth later.

However, a beginner will not pay too much heed to the actual par and will sort out his own standard. Failing to make par is depressing and the beginner must play to his ability and not attempt more than he can cope with.

A reasonable starting point is to try and make a 4 on the par 3's, a 5 on the 4's and a 6 on the par 5. This will give you one extra shot on each hole, in which to reach the green. This removes some of the pressure to 'let fly' with each shot in order to reach the green in regulation. If you can manage this on a par 72 course you can be looking at a score of 90 – not bad for starters! Although you probably won't manage to play to your 'Personal Par' initially, you should still manage to get round in under 100 and that is the magical score that most beginners want to beat. Don't let your ego control the game, allow your brain to take the strain.

GOOD MANNERS

If you find that your game is following behind the match in front, say by one clear hole, then again it is good manners to ask the match behind to play through. How often one hears, with regard to slow play, that it is always the 'four in front'. It might just be you, so either make an effort to speed up or wave the people you are holding up through.

Pacing Distances

The average person's step is as near a yard as makes no difference and here is a very rough guide to 'Mr Average'. Don't take this as gospel, you will still need to measure your own.

Men	Loft	Distance
Driver	12°	220 yds
3 wood	16°	200 yds
5 wood	23°	180 yds
3 iron	23°	180 yds
4 iron	27°	170 yds
5 iron	31°	160 yds
6 iron	35°	150 yds
7 iron	39°	140 yds
8 iron	43°	130 yds
9 iron	47°	120 yds
Wedge	52°	100 yds
Sand Iron	58°	80 yds

Ladies	Loft	Distance
Driver	12°	190 yds
3 wood	16°	170 yds
5 wood	23°	150 yds
3 iron	24°	140 yds
4 iron	28°	130 yds
5 iron	32°	120 yds
6 iron	36°	110 yds
7 iron	40°	100 yds
8 iron	44°	90 yds
9 iron	48°	80 yds
Wedge	52°	70 yds
Sand Iron	58°	50 yds

Playing the Course

This is the second stage of learning to play golf. You have learnt the basics of how to swing the club on the practice ground. Now you have to sit an examination on the golf course. The course will present you with eighteen different problems and you have to apply yourself to them.

At this point, look up the length of the hole and decide where the main trouble lies. Tee the ball on the same side of the teeing ground as the trouble, to give the feeling of hitting away from the problem.

If there is a great deal of trouble on both sides of the fairway and distance is not the problem, it might be sensible to drop down to a long iron, as any side spin imparted is not so great as with a wooden club. This is not 'chickening out' but playing the percentages. When playing safe, always use your full swing and don't try to steer the ball or swing the club softly, this will probably cause quitting on the shot.

The tee shot, particularly the first one of the day, can set the mood for the round, so give this shot 101% concentration and never hurry it. Nothing builds confidence more than getting away to a good start.

Teeing off

When you stand on the teeing ground, always find a nice flat area for your feet and the ball. This might appear obvious but do take great care in teeing the ball. Golf is difficult enough without starting from an uneven lie. You are permitted under the rules to tee the ball up to two club lengths behind the two tee markers.

RULE BOOK

If when starting a hole you play from the wrong place, you will incur two penalty strokes and then you must play from the correct place. Should you complete the hole without realising the mistake then you are disqualified. In match play your opponent can ask you to replay the shot from the correct place without penalty.

Iron Shots

Whereas with the wooden clubs power is the name of the game, with iron clubs it's all down the accuracy. You now have to hit the green and get the ball as close to the flag as you can, so as you can see these clubs, particularly the shorter irons, are the scoring clubs. It is therefore vital that you choose the right club for the distance required.

Firstly, by using the practice ground, you have to discover how far each of the iron clubs makes the ball travel.

The simplest way to discover this distance is to start with the six iron and hit about 20 balls. You can then pace out the distance from the hitting point to the middle of the pile of balls. This will give a reasonable idea of the distance you can hit with this club. Each iron club is different by 4 degrees from the one on either side of it and this 4 degrees represents approximately 15 yards, so by using the six iron as the standard it is quite easy to work out the other clubs.

Armed with this knowledge, you can find markers on the course where your normal tee shot will finish, say a tree or a bunker. You can then pace out the distance from that landmark to the green, to establish how far to hit the ball, then select the corresponding club. These distances from your markers can be jotted down on a score card or note book and kept in your golf bag for future reference. A tournament professional would never dream of going out to play a tournament round without his yardages. You will often see a player and his caddy on television, referring to 'the book' before hitting the shot. Other factors do have to be taken into account, such as whether the shot is down wind or into the wind, but it is essential to have the distance first.

FAULT-FINDER

Many mis-hits are caused by indecision in club selection. Make sure you have done your groundwork before you select your club.

Another factor to consider when playing to the green is where the trouble lies. If there is a stream in front of the green, then it is advisable to take extra club (less lofted), and endeavour to hit the ball to the back of the green or perhaps even slightly over it. There is a penalty shot for lifting the ball from a water hazard and golf is hard enough without having to add on shots that you haven't even hit. On the other hand, if you don't feel confident that the green can be reached, play the shot you're happy with and lay the ball up short of the hazard, leaving a relatively short shot to the flag.

By taking sufficient club to clear the hazard, or by laying up, you can effectively eliminate it from your mind. Conversely if there is, for example, an out of bounds or some trees behind the green, then a shorter iron would be the order of the day, as this would bring the ball down on to the green short of all the trouble. If the flag favours one side of the green or the other, always play to the safe side, or the wide side. This will usually leave the easiest chip or pitch for the next stroke. Always play the percentages, there is nothing cowardly about it.

Putting

It is always advisable to hit a few balls to loosen up before going out on to the course. This is especially so with the putter, in order to get the speed and feel of the greens. Don't start with the short ones, hit a few longer putts to establish a smooth stroke and get the feel of the pace of the greens. Then move in closer to the hole and build up confidence, by holing the shorter ones, say two to three feet.

Don't practise for too long before playing or you risk losing concentration. Remember the shortest putt counts for the same as a full blooded hit with a wood, so give it full concentration and don't treat it lightly. The game is full of stories of missed short putts that looked so easy that the player just took them for granted. Hale Irwin, twice winner of the U.S. Open cost himself a chance of tie-ing for the 1983 Open Championship at Royal Birkdale by missing from 2″ and Craig Stadler may well have changed the outcome of the 1985 Ryder Cup by missing from 18″.

GOOD MANNERS

Never, ever attempt to play a shot if the match in front is not out of range or you think there is a possibility of hitting someone with the ball. Apart from anything that you might do to someone else it will only serve to distract your concentration for your own shot.

Playing in Different Weather Conditions

When playing golf, you have to be adaptable, as the weather does not always lend itself to good scoring. Unless the golf course becomes flooded, or there is perhaps the risk of lightening, the golfer is not allowed to shelter when playing in a competitive situation. The show must go on – so to speak.

In the rain
When playing golf in the rain, being prepared with the right equipment can help to combat these conditions.

A good quality waterproof suit is a must. These are well designed and allow you to swing freely, even though you are now playing with an extra layer of clothing. The modern materials breathe, so you don't perspire and become hot and sticky. A professional will advise you on the best one to buy as he will carry a good stock.

Next you need an umbrella. Apart from keeping you dry, you can carry a towel in the umbrella ribs and use this to dry your hands and the grips on your clubs. As wet grips are a major problem, the towel is essential. Golf gloves too, become soggy and slippery when wet, but the all-weather glove can help here. It is of synthetic material not leather, it absorbs the moisture and is less expensive. It is a good idea to have one of these gloves in your golf bag at all times, in case you get caught in the rain during the round.

Good footing too is very important. During the round, keep the spikes on your shoes free of grass and other debris by running a tee peg over them periodically. There is nothing more irritating when playing in the wet than making a good swing and having the footing slip from under you. When playing in the rain, remember that everyone will be finding it just as difficult, so play sensibly. Don't attempt any risky or fancy shots, stick to the safe ones, the ones you know you can play.

For the fairway shots don't be afraid to use a more lofted club when the grass is wet, as the grooves on the blade fill with moisture and the ball will tend to skid off the club. Once again, on the approach shots, go with the lofted club. The running shot will be more difficult to judge, as the bounce on the wet grass will be unpredictable. It may skid or snag in the wet grass. Remember there are no bad bounces in the sky.

RULE BOOK

Casual water; ground under repair: You may lift a ball clear, if the conditions interfere with your stance or the ball, without penalty. Take the free drop at the nearest point of relief not nearer the hole. On the green, the ball may be moved so that you may have a clear putt. Should the ball be in a hazard you may lift it clear of the water and drop it still in the hazard without penalty. If however the bunker is completely full of casual water, then the ball is dropped outside the trap under penalty of one stroke. The original spot where the ball lay must be kept between you and the hole. A ball in a stream or water hazard is lifted clear under penalty of one stroke.

On the putting green you will have to stroke the ball more firmly as the water will drag on the ball and the burrow will be reduced. The wet grass will hold the ball on its line just as will the firmer stroke.

In the wind

Playing in the wind is also extremely difficult, but as with the rain, remember that everyone is experiencing difficulty. When playing into the wind the general tendency is to try to hit the ball harder, whereas in fact the opposite is the best policy. By attempting to swing more smoothly, you will find it easier to control your balance and achieve greater control over the swing. Obviously, extra club has to be taken to counteract the wind.

Downwind has its advantages, as the ball will fly further. A more lofted club will travel further, as you will put the ball higher in the air and so take more from the wind. There is a disadvantage, however in the shorter pitches when the ball will roll further, since the wind eliminates a lot of the backspin. It can turn par fives into fours and so make it easier to play to your handicap.

Crosswinds are extremely difficult and as a general rule, never try to fight the wind, always use it to your advantage. The most difficult of the crosswinds is when it blows on to the flat of your back as this will tend to force you on to your toes, making it very difficult to control the overall swing. You get blown into the ball, which will make you inclined to cut across the ball, making it travel from left to right.

FAULT-FINDER

When pitching or putting into the wind, attack the hole a little more, as the ball will definitely stop more quickly.

Competition

In order to compete, whether in competitions or just matches with friends, you now require a handicap. Basically, you have to be a member of a golf club to achieve this. Golfing societies do employ the system but less strictly. To play in Open Competition this type of handicap might not be acceptable.

The Handicap

To achieve a handicap, most clubs ask that three scores are returned and an average of these three scores is taken. This average is compared to the par for the course and the difference will represent the player's handicap.

Stroke Play

An 18 hole score is where each shot is recorded for each hole and the player is competing against the course. His score will then be compared to that of his fellow competitors and obviously the lowest score with handicap deducted (the net score) will be deemed the winner. The maximum handicap for male players is 28 and for ladies, 36. As the player improves and his net score becomes under the par for the course, the golf club handicapping committee will reduce the handicap accordingly.

RULE BOOK

If you play the wrong ball in stroke play, you will incur a two stroke penalty and then play the correct ball. In match play you would lose the hole. (Should the ball be in a hay-yard then no penalties occur in either situation).

Match Play

This game is the most popular among club golfers. This is where two golfers will compete directly against one another and individual holes are won and lost by the lowest score. The player with the higher handicap will receive ¾ of the difference in the handicap (his against his opponent's) and the strokes received will be taken on the appropriate holes as marked on the club score card (stroke index). Again a net score will be obtained and if this is lower than the opponent, then that player will be 1 up and so on. When a player is more holes 'up' than there are holes left to play he is the winner. For example, a player will have won his match 3 and 2 when he is three holes up and there are only 2 holes left to play. This type of game is not quite so taxing, as a really bad hole only loses you one hole. In a stroke play event it can ruin the whole score.

There are even different forms of match play.

Foursomes

This is where two players will play one ball, hitting the ball alternately, on each hole and also taking alternate tee-shots. The handicap allocation is 3/8 of the difference of the joint handicaps.

Fourball Golf

This is where two teams of two players will play match play, each player playing his own ball and the low ball of each team will count for each side. The normal holes up, holes down, format will then apply. The handicap system here is where each player will take ¾ of the difference in the handicap from the lowest handicap player.

When competing you have to learn the mental side of golf and really a whole book could be written on this subject. Most players find match play less demanding, as bad shots can quickly be forgotten. Whereas in stroke play each and every shot has to be

---

RULE BOOK

If you hit the ball out-of-bounds you will play 3 off the tee (a 2 stroke penalty of stroke and distance). You may stand out-of-bounds to play a ball that is in bounds.

written down. The classic expression of one shot at a time really does apply here. How often we hear a player comment that he only needed to make a 5 at the last hole to beat his handicap and he managed to take an eight or even worse. The real mental mistake here is that his mind is already on the green, yet his body is on the tee. You should trust the swing that has carried you for seventeen holes and not let your mind run riot. You will also become over protective and the swing will tend to become jerky and short. Even the top tournament player will tell you that under pressure, he has to remind himself to complete the back swing.

Coping with pressure

Pressure is really the fear of failure or embarrassment and this is why most people don't produce their best golf in a tight situation. Imagine walking along a plank of wood 6″ wide resting on the floor. Any problems? Of course not! Now put the plank 6′ in the air between two ladders – still no problem, but I bet you're not quite so happy about walking along it. Now put the plank 60′ up in the air between two buildings. How do you feel now? Remember it's the same plank and you are the same, so what's the problem. It's knowing what will happen if you fail that causes the fear. That's PRESSURE!

How can you combat this tight feeling under pressure? By concentrating fully on the shot to be played and by not taking stupid risks – by playing sensibly and keeping a cool head.

To keep the high scores on a hole down, always play safely, particularly when a bad shot or a mistake has been made. Get the ball back in play as soon as possible and don't try the miracle shot – it never comes off when you appear to need it most. Always accept when you have made a mistake and realise that it will probably cost you a shot to a par, but do your best to make sure it is only the one.

Match play tactics

Match play tactics will differ as you will often have to take into account your opponent's situation. For example, if he has knocked his ball off the course – out of bounds – he will have two penalty shots – stroke and distance – to add to his score. It would then be very silly for you to do the same. A real safety shot is what is required here, even to the extent of deliberately playing for a safe one over par score.

On the other hand if you are one down and one to play, a risk may well have to be taken. A halved hole is of no use – only a win is any use. Better to die trying to win the hole and perhaps lose by two, than to play lamely for a 5 when your opponent looks as if he will do no worse than a five. You will have to let the circumstances dictate your tactics.

On the green, the putt may have to be struck extra boldly to make sure of at least reaching the hole, as the return putt might well be of no consequence. Lee Travino has always stated that 90% of putts that finish short won't go in the hole (you have to agree but the same also applies to the other 10%!).

Practice

Players with limited time would obviously prefer to play than to practise, but how good a player you want to become will depend on the effort you are able to put in. However this does not mean standing on the practice tee for hours, just beating golf balls. How often does one hear in the clubhouse after a round a golfer say, "I hit 200 balls yesterday and today I played worse – practice is just a waste of time." If it was purely quantity then we would all be great players.

Before starting a practice session always have an objective in mind – even if it is only to become accustomed to the unfamiliar feeling of an adjusted grip. Always work on the fundamentals – those first five points of the sequence to achieve the good 'set-up' and try to make a nice smooth controlled swing with a medium iron. Don't stand there with a driver, or your practice will end up as a long hitting competition, with you as the loser. You want quality and not quantity.

An excellent exercise to develop the swinging effect is to start a session by hitting 6 or 7 iron shots with your feet together. Gradually widen your feet, until full width but try to retain the feeling in your hands and arms. It is surprising just how far the ball will travel, as you achieve good rhythm and timing. By all means end up with on or two wooden club shots as the rhythm will get faster. A lot of time should also be spent practising the short game. This can save lots of shots and is good practice for recovering from shots that miss the target.

Pre-round practice
This is basically to loosen up and get the golfing muscles moving again. Start with the wedge (not the driver as a full blooded swing with cold muscles can cause damage!) and hit half a dozen shots with each club, building up to the woods and your fullest swing. Again, be aware of checking all the points such as alignment etc. just in case any little faults may have crept in. Better to find them before going to the course.

After the full shots, try a few putts just to regain feel. All this will take about fifteen minutes, so try and get to the course a little earlier, then you will be nicely prepared for the opening tee shot and as mentioned earlier, there is nothing nicer than getting away to a good start.

Post-round practice
This is not always possible for the golfer but as faults
can occur during the round, or one particular club has
caused a problem, it is good to try and restore
confidence as quickly as possible, by trying to
eliminate the fault. If you have trouble putting things

GOOD MANNERS

1. Always be ready to play when it's your turn.
2. Don't wait to select a club until it's your turn to play.
3. Don't leave your clubs at the front of the green.
4. The first person to hole out should retrieve the flagstick, ready to put it back in the hole when the final player holes out.
5. Don't mark your scorecard or have discussions on the green; do that on the next tee.
6. After you have played off the teeing ground, put your club back in the golf bag while the rest of your match are hitting off and be ready to leave the tee as soon as everyone has played.
7. Take all the time you need over your shot, including the practice swing, but do walk at a reasonable pace between shots.

right by following the guide lines, ask a qualified instructor to have a quick look at you. The longer the fault persists the more you are practising that fault.

In general terms don't practise just to satisfy your CONSCIENCE. It is best to feel in the mood, otherwise your concentration will be poor and not much can be achieved.

A really good aid, particularly in the winter months, is to swing a weighted club. This will have to be done slowly as you don't want any pulled muscles. It keeps the golfing muscles loose and free at a time of year when they are inclined to get lazy due to lack of play.

Putting practice
With putting practice, try to make a competition out of it by putting with your friends as this creates the 'on course' conditions and the pressure that goes with them. So many people practise putting aimlessly, by just knocking balls at the hole. Practice can even be carried out at home. Putting practice can be carried out on the carpet, as long as there isn't too much pile and the ball is allowed to roll.

Golfer's Phrasebook

A

Ace
A hole in one stroke.

Address
The position the player assumes before swinging the golf club (set-up).

Air shot
Missing the ball completely.

Apron
The closely mown area immediately before the green, also called the fringe.

Albatross
A score of three under the par of the hole. Can only be achieved on a par 4 or par 5.

B

Banana ball
A shot that travels dramatically from left to right, (a slice).

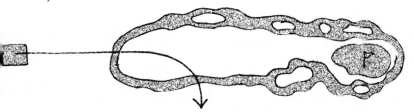

Back spin
Spin imparted on the ball to make it stop quickly on arriving at the green.

Ball position
Where the ball is placed relative to the feet in the set-up.

Borrow or Break
The amount of slope on the putting green that the player has to allow for.

Birdie
A score one under the par of the hole.

Bogey
Traditionally this in Britain has been another name for a par. However, American terminology now classes this as a one over par score.

Buried lie
This refers to a ball embedded in its own impression in a bunker.

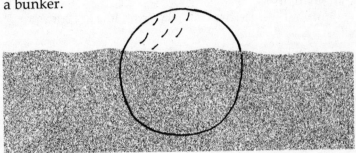

Bunker
A depression in the ground filled with sand.
Burn
A Scottish stream.

C

Caddie
A person who carries the golfer's clubs.
Carry
The distance the ball flies from where it is struck to where it first hits the ground.
Chip
A short shot played from the edge of the green.
Casual water
An accumulation of water that is not part of a water hazard and the player is permitted to take relief without a penalty stroke.

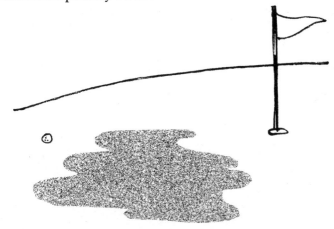

Club face
The area of the club that makes contact with the ball.

D

Dead (or stone dead)
When the ball is so close to the hole, the putt is regarded as a formality.

Divot
The piece of grass removed by the player when executing the shot.

Driver
The longest club the player has, used to start the hole at most par 4 and 5 holes.

Dormie
An expression in match play, where the player is as many holes 'up' as there are holes left to play. In other words he cannot lose.

Dog-leg (hole)
A hole that bends to the right or to the left.

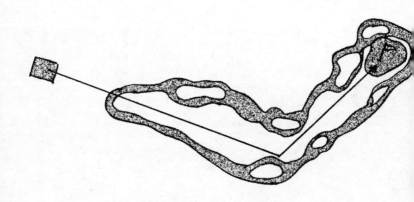

Double-bogey
A score two over the par of the hole.
Draw
A shot that moves from right to left in flight.

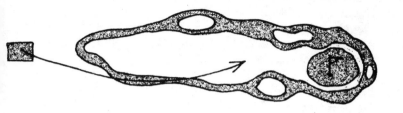

Duffer
A slang term for a player who is not particularly good.

E

Eagle
A score two under the par of the hole.

F

Fade
A ball that moves from left to right in flight.

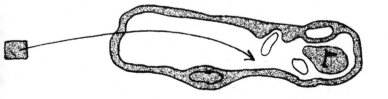

Fairway
The area between the tee and the green that is always kept mown.

Fore
A warning to another player that a ball is going to land close or possibly hit him.

Flagstick (pin)
A pole that is placed in the hole so that the player can see where the hole is located.

Flier
A ball that travels further than normal, as there is no spin on the ball. This happens from the rough when grass gets between the ball and the grooves in the club head or when the grass is wet.

Fourball
Two teams of two players each playing their own ball.

Foursome
Two teams of two players and each team plays one ball. The players play alternate tee shots and alternate shots on each hole thereafter.

Fried eggs (lie)
A slang expression for a ball buried in a bunker.

G

Green
The closely mown surface that the hole is cut in and on which the players putt.

Grip
The manner in which the club is held and also the material that is fitted to the club that the player will hold.

Green fee
The money that one pays to play as a visitor on the golf course.

H

Hook
A ball that curves drastically from right to left in flight.

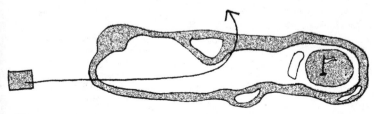

Honour
The person who tees off first on each hole according to who won the previous hole.

Handicap
The system that allows players of different standards to compete against each other.

Hazard
An area of ground that will cause the player a bother, ie. a stream or bunker.

Heel (of the club)
The part of the club head nearest the hosel.

Hosel

Heel

Hosel
The part of the club where the shaft and the club head join.

I

Insert
The plastic piece that is fitted in the face of a wooden club.

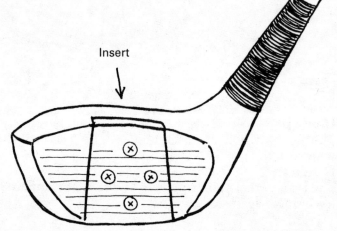

Insert

L

Loft
The amount of degrees in the face of a golf club that will control the distances the ball will travel.

Irons

1-15° 2-18° 3-21° 4-24° 5-27° 6-31° 7-35° 8-39° 9-43° PW-48° SW-

Woods

1-11°   2-13°   3-16°   4-18°   5-21°

Lip
The rim or edge of the hole. Also the edge of a bunker.
Links
The name used to describe a seaside golf course.
Originally it described where the sea and the land met.
Lie
Position of the ball on the turf, (good or bad).

M

Match play
Calculating the score of a game by holes won and lost.
Medal play
Competition where the player records each shot he makes for the eighteen holes.

N

Net score
The score the player makes after he has deducted his handicap.
Nineteenth
The bar in the clubhouse!!

O

Out-of-bounds
When the golfer hits his ball off the golf course.
Overclubbing
When the player hits his ball too far or over the green, ie. he hits a 6 iron when a 7 iron would have been enough.

P

Par

The score that the scratch handicap player is supposed to score on a hole.

Penalty stroke

A stroke (or strokes) added to a player's score when he has infringed the rules.

Playing through

When a group is holding up the match behind by playing too slowly they will ask the match behind to pass or play through.

Pull

A ball that flies straight left of the target.

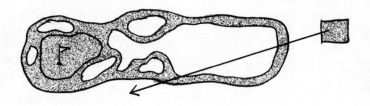

Push

A ball that flies straight to the right of the target.

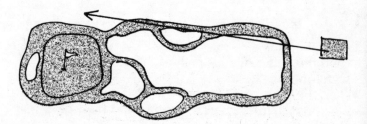

Preferred lie
A club rule that permits a player to improve his lie on the fairway without penalty. Usually in the winter time or if the fairways are in bad condition.
P.G.A
Professional Golfer's Association.
Provisional ball
A shot played after the previous ball is thought to be lost or out of bounds.

R

R & A (Royal and Ancient Golfclub)
The governing body of the amateur game based at St. Andrews, Scotland.
Rub of the green
An expression used to describe a lucky bounce or ricochet.

S

Scratch (handicap)
A player who receives no handicap allowance.
Slice
A shot that curves considerably from left to right.

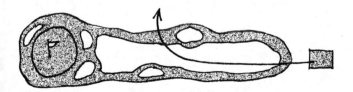

Sole
The bottom of the club head.

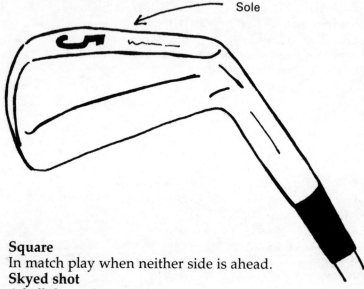

Sole

Square
In match play when neither side is ahead.
Skyed shot
A ball that is hit very high.
Short game
The part of golf played on or around the green.
Standard Scratch Score (S.S.S)
The rating of a golf course according to its difficulty.
(Always marked on the scorecard).
Shank
The worst shot in golf!! The ball is struck on the hosel
of the club and the ball goes straight right along the
ground.

T

Tee
A peg in which the ball is placed at the start of each hole. Also the area of ground where the hole begins (teeing ground).

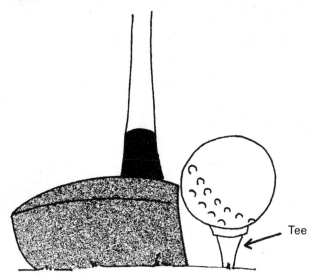

Tee

Texas wedge
A shot played from off the green with a putter.
Top
When the ball is hit above its centre and it scuttles along the ground.

Toe (of the club)
The part of the clubface farthest from the hosel.

Toe

U

Underclub
Using a club that will not allow the ball to reach the target, ie. using a 7 iron when the distance required needed a 6 or 5 iron.

Unplayable lie
When the lie is so bad or awkward that there is not a shot 'on' and the player has to take relief under penalty.

W

Waggle
The preliminary movement of the club just before the swing is made.

Whipping
The thread around the neck of the wooden headed golf club.

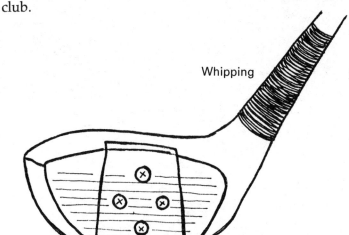

Whipping

Winter rules
A club rule that allows the player to lift, clean and place his ball on the fairway within 6 inches of where it originally lay but not closer to the hole.

Y

Yips
A nervous jab at the ball with a putter particularly on short putts.